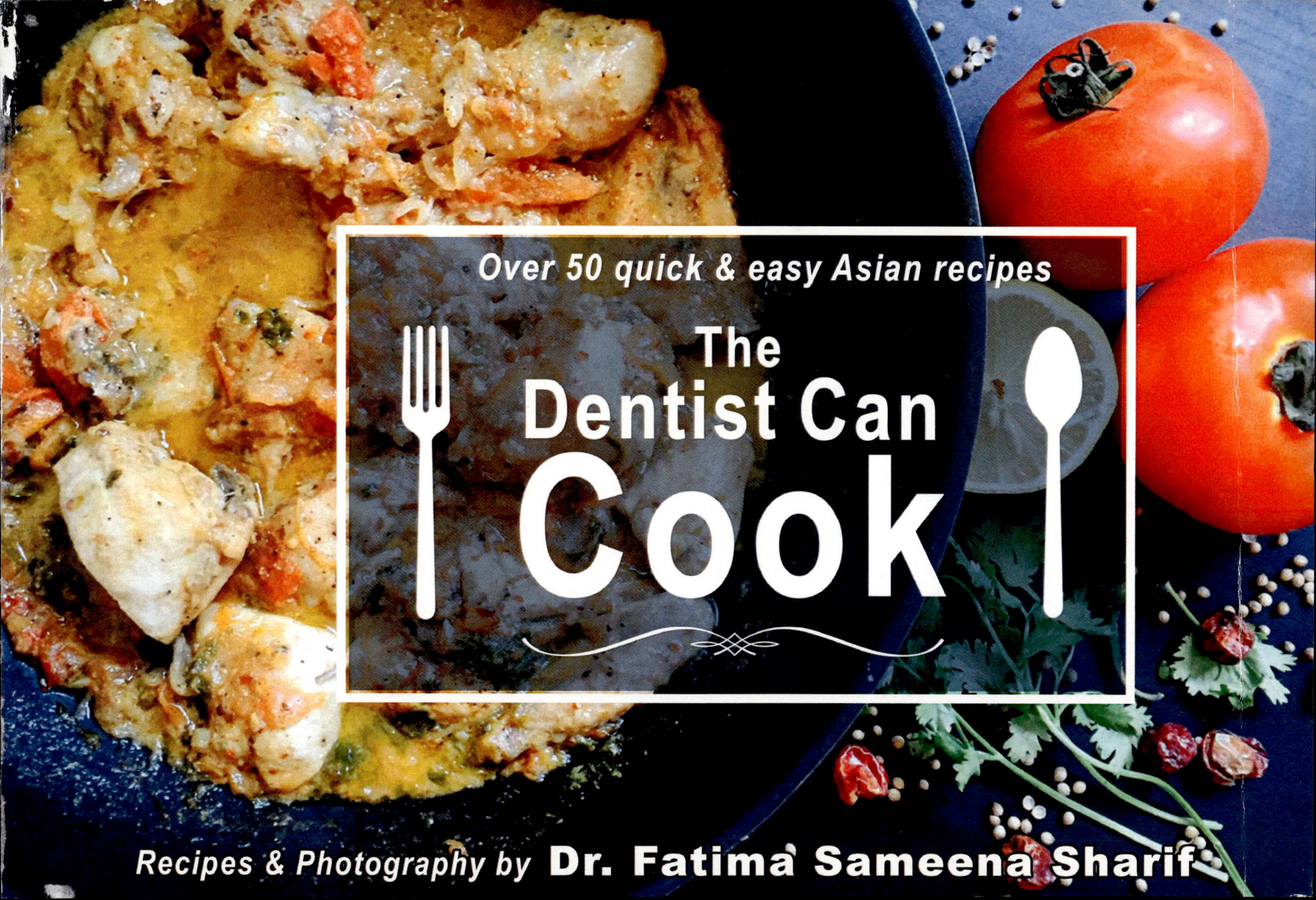
Over 50 quick & easy Asian recipes
The Dentist Can Cook
Recipes & Photography by Dr. Fatima Sameena Sharif

First published in India in 2017 by Invincible Publishers

ISBN: 978-93-86148-66-7

Corporate Office: G - 120, Sushant Lok III, Sector 57, Gurgaon-122002
Registered Office: Opposite Kasturba Ashram, Radaur Distt Yamuna Nagar, Haryana- 135133
Tel: +91 124 4273677, +91 959966 7779

About the Author

Dr. Fatima Sameena Sharif is a dentist by profession, a wife and a mother of two toddlers. She was born in Karachi, Pakistan, and has achieved her B.D.S degree in her homeland. During the course of her masters, she had to relocate to Saudi Arabia with her husband. Due to finite job opportunities in her residing city, she became a full-time mom and planned to start a food blog. Shortly afterwards, she started to click such enticing food photographs without which her blog would have been deficient.

Therefore, to share her day-to -day recipes with her followers, a platform was created to showcase her cooking talents.

The title 'The Dentist can Cook' was inspired by numerous people in our Indo-Asian society, who go by the saying that if a woman devoted half her life in her career, she would not be able to cook and take care of her family like a traditional Asian woman should. Women are multi-taskers; they are capable and skilled enough to take care of their professional as well as their family life, simultaneously.

This cookbook would be an inspiration to all such women, who like her, were unknown to the basics of cooking till they got married or had to cook for their family. Dr. Fatima's book consists of many swift and effortless recipes that are traditional, delicious yet less time consuming and require minimal performance. She has made an effort of compiling over 50 recipes that feature a marvelous range of tastes, textures and aromas from Asia and the Middle East. It encourages cooking fresh, homemade meals rather than takeaways. Easy to follow recipes, with a thorough step-by-step pictorial guide when required.

Dr. Fatima Sameena Sharif
Email: Sameena_21@hotmail.com
Instagram: Dentistcancook
Blog: Dentistcancook.niammy.com

Acknowledgment

The completion of this book could not have been possible without the participation and assistance of many people. I would like to thank my parents, my husband and my entire family for their unconditional support. A special thanks to my sister-in-law, Sana, who was my mentor in the kitchen.

I would like to express my deep appreciation to Dovile Diofky for giving me the opportunity to create a food blog and for always encouraging me.

Last, but not the least, I would like to thank my publisher, Invincible Publishers, for helping me with the process of publishing and bringing it out so beautifully.

INTRODUCTION TO SPICES AND LENTILS USED IN THE BOOK

Maash daal/ white lentils

Masoor daal/ red lentils

Chana daal/ split chickpeas

Sabut masoor/ brown lentils

Moong daal/ yellow lentils

Red chili button

INTRODUCTION TO SPICES AND LENTILS USED IN THE BOOK

Sabut dhaniya/coriander seeds

Kalonji/ Black seeds

Badiyan ka phool/Star aniseed

Rai dane/ Mustard seeds

Badi ilaichi/ Brown cardamom

Tejpata/ Bay leaves

INTRODUCTION TO SPICES AND LENTILS USED IN THE BOOK

Dar cheeni/ Cinnamon stick

Saunf/ Fennel seeds

Sabut kali mirch/ Black pepper corn

Ilaichi/ Cardamom

Long/ Cloves

Zeera/ Cumin seeds

CONTENTS

Appetizers/ snacks

Salads

Soups

Chutneys and Raita

Rice

Vegetarian

Chicken

Mutton

Desserts

APPETIZERS/
SNACKS

1. CHANA CHAAT (Chickpea Snack)

CHANA CHAAT (Chickpea Snack)

Chana chaat is a spicy, tangy and savory snack made of potatoes, chickpeas, tamarind chutney, yogurt and spices.

Method:

- In a pot on medium heat, add chickpeas, potatoes, red chili powder, chaat masala, tamarind syrup and salt. Pour in half cup of water and let it cook for 5 minutes till just a few tbsp of water is left.
- Keep onion, tomato, green chili, sweet tamarind chutney and yogurt in separate bowls.
- In a plate, add the chickpeas and potatoes, top it with yogurt and tamarind chutney followed by onion, tomatoes and coriander leaves. Sprinkle chaat masala.

How to make tamarind syrup? Add two tbsp of tamarind pulp with one glass of water and let it boil for 10 minutes. Filter the tamarind syrup by removing tamarind pulp and seeds.

Servings : 4

Preparation time: 20 minutes

Ingredients:

500g boiled chickpeas
2 medium boiled potatoes cut into cubes
1 tsp red chili powder
1 tsp chaat masala
4 tbsp sour tamarind syrup
1 ½ tsp salt
½ cup water
1 small tomato chopped
1 green chili chopped
1 small onion chopped
1 cup blended yogurt
Sweet tamarind chutney
Fresh coriander leaves chopped for garnishing
Chaat masala to sprinkle

2. DAHI BAREY

DAHI BAREY

Dahi Barey is one of the most popular Indo-Asian snacks. Barey are blended lentils which are deep fried and soaked in Dahi (sweetened yogurt).

Method:

- Soak the lentils in water for 4 hours. Drain the water. Blend the lentils along with onion, green chili, salt, garlic and water till a smooth batter is formed.
- Add baking powder to the batter and mix. Deep fry 1 tsp batter in medium hot oil till they become round and golden. Keep aside the Bareys so that they reach room temperature.
- Soak the bareys in water for 15 minutes.
- Meanwhile, mix together yogurt, sugar and milk in a bowl.
- Gently squeeze the soaked Bareys to drain excess water. Place it in the yogurt bowl. Refrigerate for about an hour or more.
- Sprinkle chaat masala and serve.

Servings : 3-4

Preparation time: 30 minutes

Ingredients:

¼ cup Maash daal/ white lentils
¼ cup Moong daal/ yellow lentils
1 medium sized onion
1 green chili
1 tsp salt
2 garlic cloves
¼ cup water
¼ tsp baking powder
1 ½ cup yogurt
½ cup milk
6 tsp sugar or more to taste
Chaat masala to sprinkle
Oil to fry

3. POTATO VADA

Mashed potato balls are dipped in chickpea powder and deep fried. Kids are unable to resist the roundness and puffiness of these balls. Easy to make snack at tea time or when you have a party at home.

Method:

- In a bowl, add mashed potatoes, salt, chaat masala, lemon juice, red chili powder and coriander leaves.
- Mix and mould to make about 20 balls. Keep in the freezer for half-an -hour.
- In another bowl, add all the ingredients of the batter. Pour water gradually and mix to form a thick batter. Leave the bowl covered for about half-an -hour. Add baking powder to the batter before frying.
- Dip the balls in the batter and fry on medium heat till golden brown. Serve hot with ketchup/ chutneys.

Servings : 6

Preparation time: 45 minutes

Ingredients:

For the potato masala

3 large boiled potatoes mashed
1 ½ tsp salt
1 tsp red chili powder
1 tsp chaat masala
2 tbsp lemon juice
½ cup fresh coriander leaves chopped

For the batter:

1 tsp red chili powder
1 tsp chaat masala
½ tsp black seeds
1 cup chickpea powder
Water
1 tsp salt
½ tsp baking powder
Oil to fry

4. POTATO SAMOSA

POTATO SAMOSA

Potato samosa 'witch's hat' as I call it are the ultimate snack on a rainy weather. Crispy, crunchy and full of flavor, these samosas can be served with chutneys or ketchup.

I must say they are tricky, a little tough to make for the first timers. But try, try, try and you may succeed.

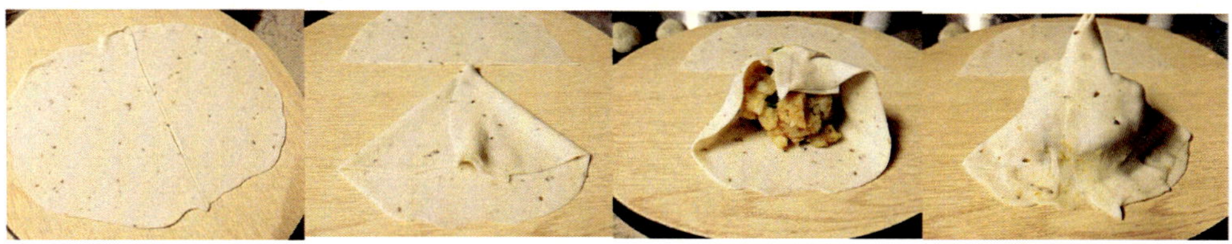

Method:

- Form a soft pliable dough with all-purpose flour, roti flour, crushed cumin seeds, salt, oil and water.
- Make 12 balls, roll them into round and thin sheets. Cut them into two and form triangles.
- Stuff the potato masala and seal the samosa like shown in the pictures.
- Freeze the samosa for an hour. Deep fry the samosas on medium heat for 5 to 10 minutes turning the samosa till they are evenly golden brown.
- Serve hot with green and tamarind chutney.

Servings : 12

Preparation time: 45 minutes

Ingredients:

3 cup all-purpose flour
3 tbsp roti flour
2 tbsp oil
1 tsp roughly crushed cumin seeds
1 ½ tsp salt
Water
Potato masala (mentioned in potato vada recipe pg 6)
Oil to fry

5. POTATO AND MEAT CROQUETTES

POTATO AND MEAT CROQUETTES

Mashed potato and minced meat croquettes are coated with bread crumbs and deep fried.

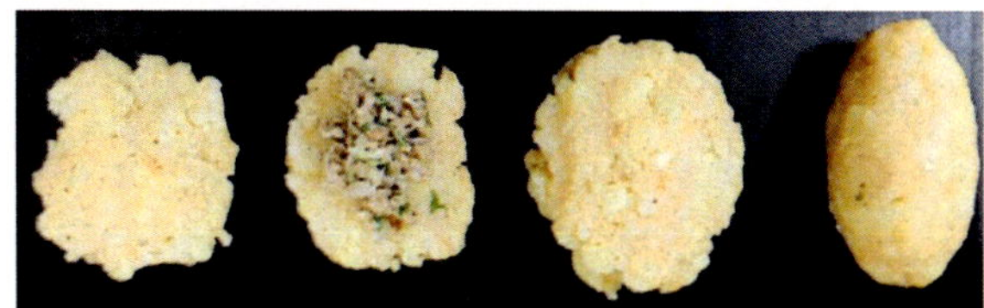

Servings : 6

Preparation time: 30 minutes

Ingredients:

For the mashed potatoes:

4 medium size boiled mashed potatoes
1 tsp red chili powder
1 tsp chaat masala
1 ½ tsp salt

For the meat mixture:

½ tsp red chili powder
1 ½ tsp garam masala
1 tsp chopped garlic
1 tsp chopped ginger
1 ½ tsp salt
1 egg beaten
½ kg minced mutton
1 large onion
1 cup fresh coriander leaves
Breadcrumbs
Oil to fry

Method:

- In a bowl, add mashed potatoes, red chili powder, chaat masala and salt. Mix and keep aside.
- In a saucepan, add oil, ginger, garlic, minced mutton, garam masala, salt and red chili powder. Sauté and add half glass of water. Let it cook completely and there should be no water left.
- Blend onion and fresh coriander leaves till they are finely chopped. They shouldn't turn into a paste. Add them to the cooled minced meat mixture.
- Mold mashed potatoes into croquettes adding meat mixture in the middle. You will form about 14 croquettes. Place in the freezer for 30 minutes.
- Dip the croquettes in the egg mixture and coat with the breadcrumbs. Place in the freezer for 30 minutes before frying.
- Deep fry on medium heat for 3 minutes turning the croquettes till they are evenly golden brown. Serve hot with ketchup/ chutney.

6. HOT SHOTS

Servings : 4

Preparation time:
30 minutes
Marination time:
4 Hours

Ingredients:

500g boneless chicken cut into small cubes

For marination:

½ tsp red chili powder
½ tsp red chili flakes
1 tbsp mustard sauce
1 tsp soya sauce
1 tbsp Worcestershire sauce
1 tsp garam masala
1 tsp coriander powder
1 tbsp lemon juice
1 tbsp white vinegar
¼ tsp black pepper powder

HOT SHOTS

Hot shots, this is what I call it, are similar to chicken nuggets. They are basically chicken pieces infused with Asian spices and covered with crumbs.

Have it as an appetizer or fill your tummy completely with these hot bites. Serve with your favorite dip, mayo or salsa.

¼ tsp white pepper powder
1 tsp garlic paste
1 tsp ginger paste
1 tsp salt

For the liquid coating:

1 cup all purpose flour
½ cup corn flour
1 tsp salt
½ tsp red chilli powder
Water to mix
Breadcrumbs
Oil to fry

Method:

- Marinate the chicken for 4 hours.
- Mix corn flour, flour, red chili powder and salt with enough water to make a smooth sticky batter. It shouldn't be too runny or else it won't stick to the chicken pieces.
- Dip the chicken pieces into the batter and then coat with breadcrumbs. Place in the freezer for an hour.
- Deep fry the chicken pieces on medium heat. Serve hot with your favorite dip.

7. POTATO WEDGES

POTATO WEDGES

Crispy and flavored potato wedges can now be easily made at home. They are a perfect side dish with roast and burgers.

Servings : 6

Preparation time:
1 hour

Ingredients:

4 large potatoes cut into wedges with the skin
4 tbsp olive oil
1 tsp garlic paste
1 tsp red chili powder
1 tsp chaat masala (optional)
1 ½ tsp salt
½ tsp black pepper powder
Oil for frying

Method:

- In a large bowl, pour olive oil and all the other ingredients and mix in the wedges. Let the flavors get through the wedges for about half-an-hour.
- Bake the wedges for 20-25 minutes at 180 degrees Celsius.
- Remove from the baking sheet and deep fry in hot oil for 2 minutes or till the wedges are golden brown and crispy.
- Sprinkle salt and serve with your favorite dipping sauce.

8. MIX VEGETABLE PAKORAS

MIX VEGETABLE PAKORAS

Pakoras are made of spinach, potato and onions combined with gram flour and spices. Crispy from the outside and soft from the inside, these pakoras are sure to satisfy your appetite.

Method:

- In a bowl, mix all the spices, baking powder and the gram flour. Whisk while gradually adding water till it turns into a slightly thick and smooth batter. Keep the batter to rest for about 15 minutes.
- Mix the vegetables in the batter.
- Put tablespoon full of batter in a wok to fry. Deep fry the pakoras on med-high heat for few minutes till they are evenly golden brown.
- Serve hot with chutneys or ketchup.

Servings : 4

Preparation time: 20 minutes

Ingredients:

1 cup spinach finely chopped
1 cup onion finely chopped
1 large potato chopped
2 cup chickpeas powder/ gram flour/ besan
1 tsp red chili powder
1 tsp coriander powder
1 tsp chaat masala
1 ½ tsp salt
1 tsp black seeds
½ tsp baking powder
Water to mix
Oil to fry

SALADS

1. BITTER GOURD SALAD

BITTER GOURD SALAD

Many don't like bitter gourd for its bitter taste, but it is used in Asian cuisine. My maternal side belongs from Sri Lanka and so my mom cooks some of the dishes of Ceylon. This bitter gourd salad recipe is a must in our house with daal and rice. The tangy crisp bitter guard with onions and tomatoes further enhance the taste of the main course meal.

Servings : 4

Preparation time: 15 minutes

Ingredients:

2 bitter gourd/ bitter melon/ karela
2 tbsp lemon juice
½ tsp red chili powder
½ tsp salt
1 onion chopped
1 tomato chopped
Oil to fry

Method:

- Wash and slice the bitter gourds discarding the core.
- Deep fry on medium heat till light brown. Allow to cool.
- In a bowl, add onions, tomato, red chili flakes, lemon juice and salt. Toss in fried bitter gourd slices.

2. VINAIGRETTE SALAD DRESSING

Healthy, nutritious and a refreshing salad to give you that instant mood lift and boost your energy.

Method:

- In a classic vinaigrette, a ratio of olive oil to vinegar is 3:1 but you can add both according to your taste.
- Take a bowl, add vinegar, olive oil, thyme, garlic, salt, black pepper and sugar. Mix well.
- Add all the vegetables and give it a stir.
- Chill for an hour before serving.

Servings : 4

Preparation time: 15 minutes

Ingredients:

½ cup cabbage chopped
½ cup carrot chopped
½ cup cucumber chopped
¼ cup sliced olives
½ cup tin pineapple pieces
½ cup tin corn
¼ cup spring onions chopped
½ cup apple chopped
2 tbsp tin red beans
2 tbsp boiled chickpeas

For the dressing:

3 tbsp vinegar
6 tbsp olive oil
½ tsp black pepper powder
1 tbsp dried thyme
½ tsp crushed garlic
¼ tsp salt
1 tsp sugar

3. COLESLAW

Chilled carrot and cabbage salad mixed with mayonnaise and yogurt. This recipe is very close to the original KFC's coleslaw.

Servings : 4

Preparation time: 20 minutes

Ingredients:

1 cup cabbage shredded
½ cup carrot shredded
2 tsp sugar
2 tbsp yogurt
3 tbsp mayonnaise
¼ tsp salt
¼ tsp black pepper powder

Method:

- In a bowl, mix together yogurt, mayonnaise, salt, black pepper and sugar.
- Add cabbage and carrot to the bowl and mix. Add more sugar if you would like to sweeten your coleslaw.
- Serve chilled.

SOUPS

1. HOT AND SOUR SOUP

HOT AND SOUR SOUP

Spicy chicken soup cooked with carrots, cabbage and bell pepper for the cold winter nights.

Servings : 6

Preparation time: 45 minutes

Ingredients:

250g boneless chicken julienne cut
1 cup cabbage sliced
1 cup carrot julienne cut
1 cup green bell pepper julienne cut
1 cup corn
1 cup spring onions sliced
5 cups chicken stock
2 tbsp hot chili garlic sauce
2 tbsp ketchup
4 tbsp vinegar
1 tsp red chili flakes
½ tsp black pepper powder
2 chicken stock cubes
2 tbsp Worcestershire sauce
1 tsp garlic paste
Splash of soya sauce
2 tbsp corn flour mixed in half cup of water
1 egg beaten
Salt to taste

Method:

- In a pot, sauté julienne chicken with garlic paste in oil on medium heat. Add all the sauces, spices, chicken stock cube, vinegar except soya sauce.
- When the chicken is half cooked, add cabbage, carrot, bell pepper, corn and soya sauce. Mix and cook for 5 minutes.
- Pour in the 5 cups of chicken stock and let it cook on medium heat for 15 minutes.
- Add beaten egg and stir vigorously. Pour in corn flour with water and stir till the soup thickens.
- Garnish with spring onions. Serve hot with crotons.

Tip: Add more chili garlic sauce for spiciness.

2. GOAT NECK SOUP

My mother's recipe of thick comfort soup made with goat neck stock and boiled vegetables- baby corn, beans, onions, carrots and mushrooms.

Method:

- In a pressure cooker, sauté the neck bones in oil, ginger and garlic paste for 5 minutes on medium heat.
- Add about 1 liter of water, black pepper powder, salt and mutton stock cube. Cook for about 20 minutes after the first whistle.
- Open the pressure cooker, add in all the vegetables including the garlic cloves and the oats. Cook for another 10 minutes with the lid closed.
- Serve hot with crotons, garlic bread and rice.

Servings : 6

Preparation time: 40 minutes

Ingredients:

700 g goat neck bones
1 cup sliced carrots
1 cup sliced mushrooms
1 cup baby corn roughly chopped
1 cup green beans cut into pieces
1 cup onions cubed
4 garlic cloves
1 mutton stock cube
1 tsp salt
1 liter water
2 tbsp oil
1 tsp ginger paste
1 tsp garlic paste
1 tsp black pepper powder
2 tbsp oats

3. CHICKEN CORN SOUP

Servings : 6

Preparation time: 40 minutes

This chicken corn soup would uplift me spiritually and physically. It's my medicinal magic soup, yet another courtesy of my mother.

Ingredients:

400g boneless chicken cut into strips
1 tsp garlic paste
1 tsp ginger paste
340g tin corn
3 tbsp corn flour
4 cups of chicken stock
2 beaten egg
2 chicken stock cube
6 tbsp oats
Salt to taste
1 tsp black pepper powder
1 cup spring onions chopped (optional)

Method:

- In a pot, sauté chicken strips in oil on medium heat with ginger, garlic and a pinch of salt and pepper. Remove from pot when the chicken is cooked and keep aside.
- In the same pot, add chicken stock, chicken stock cubes, black pepper powder, oats, corn, chicken strips and salt. Let it boil.
- Add corn flour, stir till the soup thickens. Pour in the beaten egg gradually into the pot and stir quickly so that the egg scatters in the soup.
- Turn off the stove and add spring onions.
- Serve hot with crotons.

Tip: Chicken stock can be made from chicken bones in 5 cups of water. Add 4 garlic cloves, ginger slices, 1 carrot, 1 onion, ½ cup fresh coriander leaves and 1 tsp black pepper corns. Boil till you are left with about 4 cups of water. Strain and keep the stock. You can also freeze the stock for a month or two.

CHUTNEYS
& RAITAS

1. DATE AND TAMARIND CHUTNEY

Tamarind is not only used in Asian cuisine, but you will be interested to know that it is also used in the famous Worcestershire sauce. Tamarind gives a sweet and sour twist to the chutneys. Be it pakoras, samosas or chaat, you cannot truly enjoy these savory snacks without the chutneys. They can be stored in the freezer.

Method:

- In a saucepan, boil the seeded/ unseeded tamarind pulp with 1 cup of water for 10 minutes. Filter the mixture, discarding the seeds.
- In the same saucepan, pour the tamarind water, red chili powder, cumin seeds, jaggery, dates and salt with 1 cup of water.
- Cook the mixture for 15 minutes till the date flesh and jaggery has dissolved and you have reached the desired consistency.
- Let it cool and blend the mixture.
- Store in an air tight container.

Preparation time:
30 minutes

Ingredients:

1 cup seeded/ ½ cup seedless tamarind pulp
15 ripe brown dates (add more for sweetness)
2 cups water
1 tsp cumin seeds
3/4 tsp red chili powder
½ tsp salt
½ cup grated jaggery (add more for sweetness)

2. GREEN CHUTNEY

Green chutney made of fresh coriander and mint leaves is one of the most popular chutney served in Asia with fried items like tikka, pakode and kebabs.

Method:

- Blend all the ingredients in a blender till it becomes a smooth paste. You can add green chili if you like to spice up the chutney.

Ingredients:
2 cups coriander leaves
1 cup mint leaves
1 tbsp lemon juice
1 tsp cumin seeds
2 tbsp yogurt
½ tsp salt
1 green chili (optional)

3. MINT - TAMARIND CHUTNEY

Method:

- Mix together both the chutneys.

Ingredients:
1/3 green chutney
2/3 sweet tamarind chutney

4. ZEERA RAITA

Ingredients:

1 cup yogurt
½ tsp cumin
½ tsp salt
½ tsp black pepper
¼ cup water

Method:

- Mix all the ingredients together.

5. GREEN RAITA

Ingredients:

1 cup yogurt
½ cup mint leaves
½ cup coriander leaves
½ tsp cumin seeds
¼ cup water
½ tsp salt

Method:

- Blend together all the ingredients.

RICE

1. VEGETABLE FRIED RICE

VEGETABLE FRIED RICE

This is the most basic and gratifying vegetable fried rice recipe. It can be made in no time to impress your family.

Method:

- In a wok, add a tbsp of oil. On medium flame, make scrambled egg by vigorously stirring the egg. Keep aside.
- In the same wok, add 2 tbsp of oil, sauté carrots and capsicum on low flame.
- Add garlic, salt, white pepper, black pepper, vinegar and chicken stock cube. Mix well. Cook for 3 to 4 minutes.
- Toss in spring onions, corn and scrambled egg. Cook for 2 minutes.
- Gradually add rice to the wok while stirring so that all the rice is mixed with the vegetables.
- Serve hot with any oriental Chinese curry.

Servings : 6 - 8

Preparation time: 30 minutes

Ingredients:

2 cups rice boiled
1 carrot julienne cut
1 green bell pepper julienne cut
½ cup spring onions chopped
1 egg beaten with pinch of salt and pepper
½ cup tin corn
½ tsp black pepper
2 tsp salt
1 chicken stock cube
2 tsp vinegar
½ tsp white pepper powder
1 tsp garlic paste
Splash of soya sauce
Oil

2. BROWN LENTIL BIRYANI

Servings : 5 - 6

Preparation time:
1 Hour

Ingredients:

½ cup boiled brown lentils
2 large potatoes cut into large cubes
2 tbsp oil
2 medium size onion finely sliced
1 large tomato chopped
2 cardamom
2 bay leaves
2 star aniseed
2 cloves
1 tsp black seeds
1 tsp cumin seeds
2 brown cardamom
1 cinnamon stick
1 tsp garlic paste
1 ½ tsp red chili powder
½ tsp turmeric powder
3 – 4 soaked prunes

1 small lemon sliced
Salt to taste
½ cup oil
2 cups boiled basmati rice
½ tsp yellow food color dissolved in water

BROWN LENTIL BIRYANI

Brown lentil biryani is a good alternative for the vegans who would like to taste the flavors of a traditional biryani.

Method:

- Deep fry the onions till they are golden brown and crispy. Blend the fried onions slightly. Fry the potatoes in the same oil.
- In a pot, add 2 tbsp of oil on medium heat. Add lentils, fried potatoes, crushed fried golden brown onions, tomatoes, lemon, prunes, garlic and all the spices. Cook for 10 minutes or more till the oil comes on top.
- In a big pot, layer half of rice. Spread the lentil potato mixture over it. Again cover with the remaining rice. Add ½ cup oil and food color.
- Cover with aluminum foil and cook on very low flame for 15 minutes. Serve with raita.

3. CHICKEN BIRYANI

Easy to follow recipe of chicken biryani for an amateur cook.

Method:

- Fry onions till they are golden brown. Blend the onions into a paste.
- In a pot, sauté chicken and potatoes in 3 tbsp of oil on medium heat. Add all the spices, ginger, garlic paste and chicken stock cube. Stir and mix in the onion paste and tomatoes. Add about half cup of water if the masala seems dry. Let it cook for 8 to 10 minutes.
- Blend yogurt with mint and coriander leaves. Pour this yogurt mixture followed by prunes and lemon slices. Cook for 10 minutes or more till the layer of oil is visible.
- Take a larger pot, divide the rice into two halves. Layer first half of rice and then spread all the chicken masala on it.
- Layer with the remaining rice. Add oil and yellow food coloring. Cover the pot with a foil paper and seal with the lid.
- Cook on very low flame for 15 minutes.
- Serve hot with raita and fresh salad.

Servings : 6

Preparation time:
1 Hour 30 minutes

Ingredients:

1 kg chicken pieces
2 large potatoes cut into big cubes
2 medium tomatoes chopped
2 medium onions sliced
1 cup fresh coriander leaves
1 cup fresh mint leaves
1 cup yogurt
1 small lemon sliced
2 cloves
2 bay leaves
3 cardamom
2 brown cardamom
1 tsp black seeds
1 tsp cumin seeds

Tip: Boiling the rice is the most critical step in a good biryani. Check the rice while boiling. The rice should be 80 percent cooked. It would completely cook in the pot with the chicken.

1 cinnamon stick
4 to 5 dried prunes (alu Bukhara)
1 tsp ginger paste
1 tsp garlic paste
1 ½ tsp red chili powder
½ tsp turmeric powder
1 chicken stock cube
Salt to taste
Water
½ cup oil
½ tsp yellow food color dissolved in water

4. MUTTON PULAU

MUTTON PULAU

My mother's recipe of mutton pulau is full of flavors and smells heavenly. Pulau is rice boiled in the meat stock with whole spices.

Method:

- In a pressure cooker, add meat and all the spices, ginger, garlic, mutton stock cubes and salt. Pour about 6 cups of water and cook for 15 minutes or more after the first whistle till the meat is cooked.
- Strain the meat mixture, keep the stock aside. You will get about 5 cups of stock. From the strainer, separate the meat from the spices.
- In a pot, sauté onion, ginger and garlic in oil on medium heat till they turn transparent.
- Add the meat spices and the meat stock. Let it boil on high heat.
- When the water is bubbling, add the soaked rice without any water, stir, cover with the lid for 10 - 15 minutes. Then open the lid and check the rice, when its about 80 percent cooked, cover with aluminum foil and cook on very slow flame for about 15 minutes.
- Serve hot with raita and green salad.

Servings : 8

Preparation time: 1 Hour

Ingredients:

1 kg mutton pieces with bone
2 medium size onion without peeling
2 garlic clove whole without peeling
1 inch cumin seeds
1 tbsp zeera
10 cloves
10 whole black pepper
3 bay leaves
3 cinnamon stick
10 cardamom
2 mutton stock cube
3 tsp salt
2 medium sized onion thinly sliced
1 tsp garlic chopped
1 tsp ginger chopped
3 tbsp oil
Water
4 cups basmati rice soaked for 15 minutes in water

5. SINGAPOREAN RICE

Servings : 4

Preparation time: 1 Hour

Ingredients:

2 cups boiled rice
2 cups boiled spaghetti

For the mayo sauce:

½ cup mayonnaise
2 tsp ketchup
½ tsp red chili flakes
pinch of salt

For the chicken and vegetable sauce:

1 onion chopped
½ kg boneless chicken
1 cup spring onions chopped
1 cup carrot roughly chopped
1 cup cabbage roughly chopped

SINGAPOREAN RICE

I have yet to find any link of this dish to Singapore. I did not taste it for the first time in Singapore, but in my homeland Pakistan. Singaporean rice is one of the tastiest dishes that are served in our weddings. It is the mesmerizing combination of noodles, rice, chicken, vegetables with mayo sauce.

Method:

- Prepare the mayo sauce by mixing mayonnaise, ketchup, red chili flakes and salt. Keep aside.
- In a wok, sauté onions with oil on medium heat. Add chicken, red chili flakes, cumin powder, pepper, salt, ginger, garlic, chicken stock and Worcestershire sauce. Stir for few minutes till the chicken is half cooked.
- Add all the vegetables into the wok. Splash soya sauce and pour half glass of water. Let it cook for 10 minutes.
- Mix cornflour and water together and pour into the wok. The sauce will thicken.
- Layer the rice in the dish followed by the spaghetti and chicken-vegetable sauce. Top it with mayo sauce.

1 cup capsicum roughly chopped
2 tbsp Worcestershire sauce
1 ½ tsp red chili flakes
1 tsp pepper
1 ½ tsp salt
2 tbsp soya sauce
1 chicken stock cube
1 tsp garlic chopped
1 tsp ginger chopped
1 tsp cumin powder
2 tbsp corn flour in ½ cup water
½ cup water
4 tbsp oil

VEGETARIAN

1. CHANA (CHICKPEAS) CURRY

Servings : 4 - 6

Preparation time: 30 minutes

Scrumptious and super flavorful chickpeas curry and easy to make.

Ingredients:

400g boiled chickpeas
1 large onion sliced
1 medium sized tomato cut into 4 pieces
1 green chili
2 cloves of garlic
½ tsp turmeric powder
1 tsp red chili powder
½ tsp curry powder
1 tsp coriander powder
½ tsp cumin powder
Salt to taste
½ cup water or more
Oil

Method:

- Fry the onions till they are light brown.
- Blend together fried onions, garlic, green chili, and tomato into a fine paste.
- In a pot, add 3 tbsp oil on medium heat. Add chickpeas followed by the paste and all the spices.
- Sauté for a minute and pour in the water. If you require more gravy, add water accordingly. Let it cook for 20 minutes or more on slow flame till the oil comes on surface.
- Serve hot with rotis.

2. OKRA MASALA

OKRA MASALA

Okra/ ladyfingers are one of the most loved vegetables. Okra is tossed with Indian spices to make this effortless yet finger licking meal.

Method:

- In a pot, sauté onion on medium heat in oil till they turn transparent.
- Mix in the okra with all the spices and garlic. Let it cook till the sliminess dissolves stirring occasionally.
- Add in the tomatoes and quarter cup of water. Cover and let it cook for about 10 to 15 minutes.
- Serve hot with roti/ bread.

Servings : 6

Preparation time: 40 minutes

Ingredients:

500g okra/ladyfingers sliced
1 cup onion sliced
1 cup tomato chopped
1 tsp garlic paste
1 tsp red chili powder
1 tsp curry powder
1 tsp cumin seeds
1 tsp coriander powder
½ tsp turmeric powder
1 ½ tsp salt
3 tbsp oil
Water

3. ALOO PARATHA WITH CHILI CHUTNEY

ALOO PARATHA WITH TOMATO CHILI CHUTNEY

Aloo paratha with tomato chili chutney are eaten for breakfast, lunch or dinner. They are the ultimate comfort food of the Asian community.

Method:

- In a fry pan, sauté onion on medium heat with oil. Add mashed potatoes with cumin, coriander, turmeric, chaat masala, salt, red chili flakes and garlic.
- In a kitchen aid, knead flour with the mashed potatoes mixture. Gradually add water till a slightly sticky dough is formed. Alternatively, you can knead the dough with your hands.
- Divide the dough into balls. Sprinkle flour while rolling the dough into round parathas.
- Heat a fry pan on medium to high flame. Fry the paratha on both sides with little oil till golden in color.
- Blend dried red chilies with salt, garlic, vinegar and tomato. Serve hot parathas with chutney.

Servings : 5 - 6

Preparation time: 1 Hour

Ingredients:

3 medium size potatoes, boiled and mashed
3 cups flour
1 tsp chaat masala
½ tsp cumin powder
½ tsp turmeric powder
1 tsp garlic crushed
1 onion diced
2 tbsp oil
1 ½ tsp salt
2 tsp red chilli flakes
Water
For the chutney:
4 dried red chili buttons (adjust to spice level)
Vinegar
Salt to taste
3 garlic cloves
½ tomato

4. BROWN LENTILS DAAL

BROWN LENTILS DAAL

Lentils have numerous benefits for our health. They are an excellent source of fibre, folic acid and potassium; all of which are good for our heart. They are good for pregnant women, the folate in lentils prevent birth defects. One cup of lentils provides almost 90 per cent of your folate needs for the day. Lentils decrease risk of obesity, diabetes, heart disease, cancer and constipation due to being rich in many vitamins and minerals. It is our super food!

Method:

- Boil lentils in water for about 10 -15 minutes till they are cooked on medium heat.
- In a pot, sauté onion in oil on medium heat till they turn transparent. Add garlic, tomatoes, coriander, turmeric, cumin, red chili, green chili, salt and curry leaves. Cook for 5 minutes.
- Mix in the boiled lentils and cook for 5 minutes while stirring occasionally. If you want more curry you can add half cup of water.
- Serve hot with roti/ bread.

Servings : 4

Preparation time: 30 minutes

Ingredients:
1 cup brown lentils
2 cups water
1 tsp garlic chopped
1 tomato chopped
1 onion finely chopped
5 curry leaves
1 tsp coriander powder
1 tsp turmeric powder
½ tsp red chili powder
½ tsp cumin seeds
1 green chili chopped
2 tbsp oil

5. MIXED DAAL

MIXED DAAL

Servings : 4

Preparation time:
30 minutes

Ingredients:

¼ cup moong daal/ yellow lentils
¼ cup masoor daal/ red lentils
¼ cup channa daal/ split chick peas lentils
2 garlic cloves chopped
¼ cup tomato chopped
1 green chili chopped
2 whole red button chilies
½ tsp turmeric powder
1 tsp coriander powder
1 tsp cumin powder
1 tsp red chili powder
1 ¼ tsp salt
1 chicken stock cube
3 tbsp oil
water

Method:

- In a pressure cooker, boil all three daals with 1 and a half cup of water for 15 minutes after the first whistle. If it is your first time with the pressure cooker, do check the lentils after 10 minutes to make sure the water doesn't dry out. Add more water if the lentils are not cooked, boil for another 5 to 8 minutes.
- Make the tarka mixture: Add oil, garlic, tomato, green chilies, red chilies, turmeric, coriander, cumin, salt and chicken stock with about quarter cup of water to a fry pan. Cook on medium heat.
- Add the tarka mixture to boiled lentils with half cup of water and cook for another 10 minutes on medium heat till you get the desired consistency. Add more water if you like your daal to be more soupy in texture.
- Serve hot with chapatis, boiled rice and pickle.

6. SPINACH AND POTATO CURRY

SPINACH AND POTATO CURRY

Spinach is famous for being Popeye's power food. It is rich in iron and also an excellent source of Vitamin K, Vitamin A, Vitamin C, Vitamin B2, folic acid as well as manganese and magnesium.

Method:

- In a pot, add oil and onion on medium heat. Sauté till they become transparent. Add garlic, tomatoes and spices.
- Pour half glass of water and potatoes. Cover the lid and let it cook. Meanwhile chop your spinach without the stems. Add in the spinach. Let it cook for 10 minutes with occasional stirring.
- Pour another quarter cup of water if the curry looks dry. Check if the potatoes are thoroughly cooked.
- Serve hot with bread/roti and fresh salad.

Tip: Select the dark green leaves as they contain high levels of carotenoids which serve as anti-inflammatory and anti-cancerous. Use high portions of spinach as they tend to shrink due to their high-water content after being cooked.

Servings : 4

Preparation time: 30 minutes

Ingredients:

1 onion thinly sliced
1 tomato chopped
2 garlic pods chopped
2 bunch spinach/ 4 cups chopped spinach
2 medium potatoes cut in small cubes
1 tsp red chili powder
1 tsp cumin seeds
1 tsp coriander powder
1 tsp turmeric powder
1 ½ tsp salt
4 tbsp oil
water

7. KADHI

Kadhi is a yogurt based curry made with spices and besan (chickpeas powder). Fried pakoras are added to the curry for the rich and royal texture. Kadhi is served with boiled rice.

Method:

- In a bowl, mix all the ingredients for the pakoras. Gradually add water and mix to form a thick batter.
- Heat oil on medium flame in a wok. Drop spoonful of batter in the oil. Turn the pakoras occasionally till they are evenly golden brown.
- Drain the pakoras on kitchen paper to remove excess oil. Keep aside.
- For the kadhi: Blend curd, water and gram flour together.
- In a pot, heat oil on medium flame. Add all the spices, curry leaves, garlic and salt. When the spices start to splatter, pour the blended curd mixture gradually into the pot while continuously stirring. This avoids any lumps to be formed.
- Let the curry cook for 15 minutes on low flame till the kadhi thickens. Lastly, add the fried pakoras in the kadhi.
- Serve hot with boiled rice.

Servings : 6

Preparation time: 30 minutes

Ingredients:

For the pakoras:

2/3 cup gram flour/ besan/chickpeas powder
1 tsp red chilli powder
1 tsp chaat masala
1 tsp salt
½ tsp baking powder
Oil to fry

For the kadhi:

1 ½ cup sour curd
3 tbsp gram flour/ besan/ chickpeas powder
2 tbsp oil
1 tsp mustard seeds
½ tsp fenugreek seeds
1 ½ tsp red chili powder
½ tsp turmeric powder
1 green chili finely chopped
6 fresh curry leaves (optional)
1 ½ tsp salt
1 tsp garlic
2/3 cup water

CHICKEN
RECIPES

1. CHILLI CHICKEN

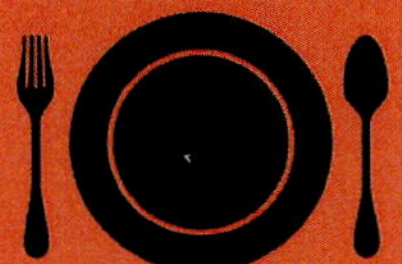

Servings : 4

Preparation time:
1 Hour
Marination time:
2 Hours

Ingredients:
500g chicken breast cut into cubes

Marination for chicken:
½ tbsp vinegar
1 tbsp soya sauce
1 tsp salt
½ tsp pepper
1 tsp garlic paste
½ tsp ginger paste
½ tsp sugar
½ cup water

For coating the chicken:
½ cup all-purpose flour
½ tsp baking powder

CHILLI CHICKEN

Chili Chicken is a perfection combination of Indo-Chinese flavor. Crispy chicken pieces are tossed with bell peppers and mushrooms in a chili sauce.

Method:

- Marinate chicken for about 2 hours. Mix together flour, baking powder and corn flour in a bowl. In a separate bowl, beat the egg.
- Coat each chicken piece first with egg and then with the flour mixture. Fry the coated chicken pieces on medium heat till golden brown and take out from the fry pan. Keep aside.
- Make the sauce by mixing soya sauce, chili sauce, red chili powder, black pepper powder, sugar, ketchup and Worcestershire sauce. Keep aside.
- In a wok, add 2 tbsp oil and sauté garlic on medium heat.
- Toss in the onions, bell peppers and green chilies. Cook for 2 minutes.
- Pour the sauce and let it simmer.
- Just before serving, pour in the corn flour mixed with water. Mix till the sauce thickens.
- Add the crispy fried chicken pieces. Heat and stir the chicken pieces with the sauces. If its added early, they won't remain crispy.
- Serve hot with fried rice or noodles.

¼ cup corn flour
1 egg beaten

For the sauce:
1 ½ tsp soya sauce
1 tsp chili sauce
½ tsp red chili powder
¼ tsp black pepper powder
½ tsp sugar
1 tbsp ketchup
1 tbsp Worcestershire sauce
2 green chilies chopped
½ tsp salt
2 garlic cloves chopped
1 onion diced
½ cup red bell pepper
½ cup orange bell pepper
½ cup yellow bell pepper
½ cup green bell pepper
½ cup sliced mushrooms (optional)
1 cup water
2 tsp corn flour
Oil

2. SPICY CHOWMEIN

SPICY CHOWMEIN

'Chow' means fried and 'mein' means noodles in the Chinese language. It is a popular Chinese dish and also famous throughout the world. Every country makes its own version of Chowmein. In Pakistan, India and Sri Lanka, spicier Chowmein is preferred. The crunchy vegetables and the spicy flavored noodles will not make you realize how much servings you have had. Be generous in making them. I have used spaghetti in this recipe, you can also make it with egg noodles.

Method:

- In a wok, sauté chicken, garlic and ginger in oil on medium heat.
- Add red chili flakes, Worcestershire sauce, black pepper, salt, chicken stock cube, ketchup and red chili sauce. Sauté for 2 minutes.
- Toss in the vegetables, add soya sauce. Pour half glass of water and let it cook for 5 minutes or more till the vegetables are half cooked.
- Mix the noodles in the wok. Fry on medium heat for 2 minutes. Serve hot.

Servings : 4

Preparation time: 30 minutes

Ingredients:

250g boiled noodles/ spaghetti
300g chicken breast julienne cut
1 cup green bell pepper julienne cut
1 cup carrot julienne cut
10 mushrooms sliced
1 small onion chopped
1 spring onion chopped
1 tsp garlic
1 tsp ginger
1 tsp red chili flakes
1 ¼ tsp salt
½ tsp black pepper powder
1 chicken stock cube
2 tbsp Worcestershire sauce
1 tbsp red chili sauce
2 tbsp ketchup
1 tbsp soya sauce
½ cup water
3 tbsp oil

3. SHISH TAWOOK

Servings : 4

Preparation time:
30 minutes
Marination time:
4 Hours

Shish Tawook is an Arabian dish originated from Turkey. Shish means skewers and tawook means chicken. Grilled boneless chicken pieces along with bell pepper, tomatoes, onions and mushrooms can be served with pita bread or rice.

Ingredients:

500g chicken breast cut into cubes
1 cup yogurt
¼ cup lemon juice
1 tsp garlic paste
½ tsp garam masala
¼ cup olive oil
2 tsp tomato paste
1 tsp dried oregano
1 tsp red chili powder (optional)
¼ tsp black pepper powder
¼ tsp turmeric powder
1 ½ tsp salt
1 cup green bell pepper cut into cubes
½ cup tomatoes cut into cubes
1 cup onion cut into cubes
1 cup whole mushrooms

Method:

- In a bowl, mix all the above ingredients with the chicken cubes. Marinate for at least four hours.
- Wet the wooden skewers and insert the chicken pieces and the vegetables.
- Place in a fry pan with little oil and cover with the lid. Cook on medium heat till the chicken is half cooked and pour the remaining marinade over the chicken.
- Now grill the chicken skewers till they are golden brown on both sides.
- Serve hot with pita bread or rice.

4. CHICKEN CREAM CHEESE TIKKA

CHICKEN CREAM CHEESE TIKKA

This tikka recipe is a mouthwatering combination of cream cheese, fresh cream, cashew nut paste and ground spices.

Method:

- In a bowl, marinate chicken cubes with salt, vinegar and white pepper for 1 hour.
- Grind cumin, coriander seeds and whole black pepper with a mortar and pestle.
- Blend together green chili, garlic cloves, ginger, red chili powder, garam masala, cashew nuts, cream, cream cheese and freshly ground spices. It should form a smooth paste.
- In the same bowl now coat the chicken with the blended paste and refrigerate for at least 4 hours.
- Preheat oven to 180 degrees Celsius. Brush the Pyrex dish with oil and place the chicken with the marination. Spread the butter over the chicken and cover with aluminum foil.
- Bake for 15 minutes and then take off the foil paper and bake for another 15 minutes tossing the chicken so that they get evenly baked on both sides.
- Serve hot with chapatis and raita.

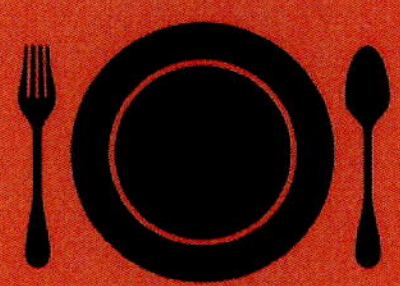

Servings : 5 - 6

Preparation time: 1 Hour

Ingredients:

500g boneless chicken cut into cubes
1 tbsp vinegar
1 ½ tsp salt
½ tsp white pepper
1 tsp cumin seeds
1 tsp whole black pepper
1 tsp coriander seeds
2 tbsp cream
3 tbsp cream cheese
1 green chili
½ tsp red chili powder
3 garlic cloves
1 tsp ginger paste
2 tbsp roasted cashew nuts
1 tsp garam masala
3 tbsp butter
Oil

5.
PESHAWARI CHICKEN KADHAI

PESHAWARI CHICKEN KADHAI

Peshawari kadhai is another specialty of Peshawar, Pakistan. Kadhai is basically a wok which is used to make this delectable dish.

Method:

- In a wok, sauté onions on medium heat with oil till they turn transparent.
- Crush black pepper, cumin and coriander seeds in a mortar and pestle.
- Add chicken, garlic, ginger, salt, pepper, chili flakes, coriander and cumin to the wok. Stir for 5 minutes.
- Add tomatoes and let it cook for 10 minutes. Pour in yogurt and cook for another 5 minutes.
- Lastly, add butter, garam masala, lemon juice and fresh coriander leaves in the wok. Leave on slow flame for 5 minutes.
- Serve hot with naan/ roti and raita. Enjoy!

Tip: If you like your Peshwari Chicken Kadhai to have that certain reddish-orange color, add 2 tsp of tomato paste. You can also use Kashmiri red chili to enhance the red color.

Servings : 4

Preparation time: 30 minutes

Ingredients:

500g boneless or 1 kg chicken with bones
1 tbsp garlic
1 tbsp ginger
1 medium size onion thinly sliced
2 large tomatoes cubed
1 tsp whole black pepper corns
1 tsp coriander seeds
1 tsp cumin seeds
1 tsp garam masala
1 ½ tsp chili flakes
1 lemon juice
2 tbsp butter
½ cup fresh coriander leaves chopped
1 ½ tsp salt
4 tbsp blended yogurt

6. CHICKEN FILLET

CHICKEN FILLET

This delicious chicken fillet is juicy, succulent and a good source of protein if you are on a diet.

Method:

- In a bowl, add all the ingredients and stir into a smooth paste.
- Coat the fillets in the marinade. Keep in the refrigerator for atleast 4 hours preferably overnight.
- Shallow fry in a frypan on medium heat with 3 tbsp oil. Turn sides and cook till golden brown.
- Serve hot with your favorite sauce.

Servings : 4

Preparation time:
20 minutes
Marination time :
4 Hours

Ingredients:

8 chicken fillets pounded with mallet
1 tsp dried basil leaves
1 tsp chopped garlic
1 tsp chopped ginger
1 tsp salt
½ tsp red chilli powder
½ tsp red chilli flakes
½ tsp paprika powder
1 tsp cumin powder
1 tsp coriander powder
1 tsp garam masala
1 tbsp mustard sauce
1 tbsp Worcestershire sauce
¼ tsp black pepper powder
1 tbsp soya sauce
1 tsp white vinegar
1 tbsp lemon juice
Oil for frying

7. ZINGER CHICKEN BURGER

ZINGER CHICKEN BURGER

Chicket fillet coated with bread crumbs, cornflakes and spices make the most crunchiest zinger burgers.

Method:

- Pound and marinate the chicken fillets for at least four hours.
- In a bowl, add all-purpose flour, corn flour and salt. Pour water gradually till it becomes a thick paste. Add hot sauce and mix. Keep aside.
- Mix together crushed corn flakes and bread crumbs. Keep separately.
- Dip the chicken fillets in the paste and then cover with the crumbs. Place in the freezer for an hour.
- Deep fry the fillets on medium heat till they turn golden brown.
- Spread mayo, ketchup and mustard sauce over the bun. Place cucumber, onion, lettuce, jalapeño and chicken fillet over the bun. Serve with fries.

Servings : 4

Preparation time:
1 Hour
Marination time :
4 Hours

Ingredients:

Marination for chicken fillets: (refer pg 66)
1 kg chicken fillet pieces
1 cup bread crumbs
1 cup corn flakes crushed
1 tsp salt
½ cup corn flour
½ cup all-purpose flour
2 tsp hot sauce
Water to mix
Oil to fry
Cucumber slices
Onion slices
Lettuce leaves
Pickled jalapeno
Mustard sauce
Mayo sauce
Ketchup

8. SPECIAL MAC & CHEESE

SPECIAL MAC & CHEESE

This is a twisted mac & cheese recipe, its little time consuming but the end product is worth the hard work. Its the perfect dish to impress your guests. I have used cheddar and mozzarella cheese. You can also use parmesan cheese.

Method:

- Preheat oven at 180 degrees Celsius. Make the chicken mixture. In a wok, melt butter on medium flame. Sauté onions till they turn transparent.
- Add chicken, ginger, garlic, chicken stock cube, mustard, red chili flakes, black pepper powder, salt, mushrooms and olives.
- Stir it and add cheddar cheese followed by flour and 700 ml milk. Cook till the sauce thickens.
- Toss the macaroni with the mixture. In a Pyrex dish, spread the chicken and macaroni mixture. Pour about 300 ml milk.
- Top it up with pasta sauce followed by Mozzarella cheese. Bake for 40 minutes till the cheese turns golden brown.
- Garnish with oregano. Serve hot.

Tip: Pasta sauce can be made at home if you don't have the ready made one. Sauté ½ cup chopped onion in 2 tbsp oil on medium heat. Add 1 tsp garlic paste, 1 tsp red chili flakes, 1 tsp vinegar, 1 cup blended tomatoes, 2 tbsp ketchup, 1 tsp sugar, 1 tsp salt, 1 chicken stock cube and 1 tsp dried oregano. Cook for 10 mins till a thick sauce is formed.

Servings : 6

Preparation time:
1 Hour 30 minutes

Ingredients:

300 g chicken cut into small cubes
50 g butter
1 onion finely chopped
½ cup olives sliced
½ cup mushrooms sliced
1 tsp red chili flakes
1/2 tsp black pepper powder
1 chicken stock cube
2 tbsp mustard sauce
1 tsp ginger chopped
1 tsp garlic chopped
50 g all-purpose flour
1 liter milk
70 g cheddar cheese roughly sliced
250g shredded Mozzarella cheese
300 g boiled macaroni
450 g pasta sauce
Dried oregano for garnishing

9. CHICKEN JALFREZI CURRY

CHICKEN JALFREZI CURRY

Tender juicy chunks of chicken cooked in spicy tomato sauce with bell peppers and onion. It can be served with plain boiled rice or naan.

Method:

- In a bowl, mix blended yogurt with turmeric, coriander and red chili powder. Toss in the bell pepper and onions. Keep aside.
- In a pot, sauté finely chopped onions till transparent on medium heat. Add chicken cubes, garlic and ginger. Cook for 5 minutes.
- Pour the blended tomatoes, tomato paste, ketchup, red chili powder, turmeric powder, coriander powder, black pepper powder, salt and lemon juice. Cook on low flame for 10 minutes.
- Add the yogurt mixture with the bell pepper and onions. Cook for another 10 minutes on low flame.
- Serve hot with boiled rice or naan.

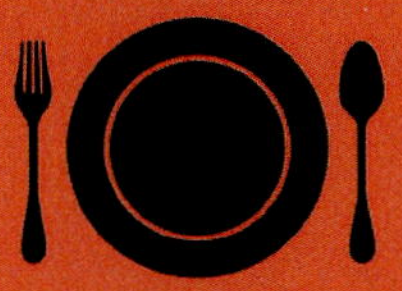

Servings : 5

Preparation time: 35 minutes

Ingredients:

For the yogurt mixture:

1 cup onion cubes
1 cup green bell pepper cubes
½ cup blended yogurt
¼ tsp red chili powder
¼ tsp turmeric powder
¼ tsp coriander powder

For the curry:

500 g boneless chicken cubes
1 tsp red chili powder
1 tsp coriander powder
3/4 tsp turmeric powder
1 ¼ tsp salt
½ tsp black pepper powder
2 tomatoes blended
2 tbsp tomato paste
1 tbsp ketchup
1 tbsp lemon juice

10. SMOKED CHICKEN TANDOORI

SMOKED CHICKEN TANDOORI

If you are planning for a bbq, impress your guests with this well-seasoned and gratifying recipe of chicken tandoori.

Method:

- In a bowl, add all the spices, yogurt, lemon juice, coriander leaves, red coloring (optional) and 2 tbsp butter. Mix till it turns into a smooth paste.
- Marinate the chicken for at least 2 hours. Overnight marination is preferred.
- Pre heat oven to 180 degrees Celsius. Coat the Pyrex dish with 2 tbsp of butter. Add the chicken pieces with the marinade coating on both sides. Cover the dish with foil paper. Bake for 30 minutes.
- Remove the foil paper. Bake on one side for 15 minutes and on the other side for another 15 minutes. Check if it is completely cooked.
- Place a piece of hot red charcoal on a foil paper in the Pyrex dish. Pour 1 tbsp oil on the coal. Cover the Pyrex dish with the previously used foil paper for about 10 minutes. This will give you smoked tandoori.
- Alternatively, the marinated chicken can be barbecued on the grill.
- Serve hot with naan and raita.

Servings : 2

Preparation time: 1 Hour

Ingredients:

1 chicken cut into 4 pieces with slits
2 tbsp lemon juice
1 tbsp garlic
1 tsp ginger
1 tbsp garam masala
1 tbsp blended coriander leaves
1 ½ tbsp paprika powder
1 tbsp coriander powder
1 tsp cumin powder
1 ½ tsp cayenne pepper
1/2 tsp ground cardamom
1 tsp turmeric
½ tsp black pepper
1 ½ tsp salt
1 cup yogurt
1 tsp red coloring (optional)
4 tbsp butter
lit coal for bbq flavour

11. PIZZA PARATHA (CALZONE)

PIZZA PARATHA (CALZONE)

Hot parathas filled with chicken and melting ooeygoey mozzarella cheese.

Method:

- Make the chicken filling first. In a pan, add oil and sauté chicken and garlic on medium heat till half cooked. Add red chili flakes, black pepper, salt and Worcestershire sauce. Pour water and bell pepper and cook for 5 minutes. Keep aside.
- If you don't know how to make paratha/rotis, you can use the frozen parathas.
- For the paratha dough, add flour and salt in the dough mixer. Gradually add water and oil. Knead till the dough bounces back and doesn't stick to the bowl. Divide the dough into 10 round balls.
- Roll each ball into a circle. Spread the pizza sauce. Add the chicken filling followed by cheese on half of the paratha. Fold like a semicircle and press the sides.
- Fry the parathas on medium heat for few minutes till light brown on both sides. Serve hot.

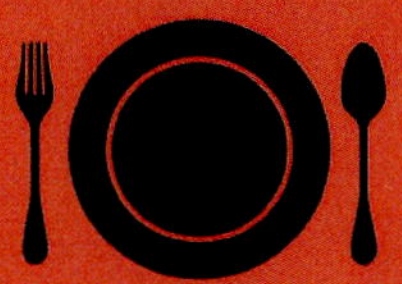

Servings : 5

Preparation time: 45 minutes

Ingredients:

300 g pizza sauce
2 cup mozzarella cheese

For the chicken filling:

400g chopped boneless chicken pieces
½ cup chopped green bell pepper
½ cup chopped olives
1 tsp salt
½ tsp black pepper powder
1 tsp red chili flakes
1 tbsp Worcestershire sauce
½ cup water
1 ½ tbsp oil

For the dough: (alternatively can use frozen parathas)

3 cups flour
1 ¼ cup water or more
1 tsp salt
1 ½ tbsp oil

12. CHICKEN TIKKA ROLL

CHICKEN TIKKA ROLL

Chunky, juicy chicken pieces infused with Indian spices wrapped in parathas.

Method:

- In a bowl, add all the above ingredients and mix with the chicken. Marinate for at least 4 hours.
- In a frypan, on medium heat, cook the chicken till the marination dries up.
- Place the lit coal in middle of the frypan over a piece of aluminum foil. Pour ½ tsp of oil on the coal and cover the lid for 15 minutes.
- Spread mayonnaise and pickled onions over the paratha. Place chicken pieces and roll it.
- Serve with mint chutney.

Servings : 4

Preparation time: 1 Hour
Marination time: 4 Hours

Ingredients:

500 g boneless chicken cut into cubes
1 cup yogurt
½ tsp turmeric powder
½ tsp cumin powder
½ tsp black pepper powder
1 tsp garam masala powder
1 tsp red chili powder
1 tsp paprika powder
1 tsp ginger paste
1 tsp garlic paste
2 tbsp oil
1 ½ tsp salt
2 tbsp vinegar
1 tbsp lemon juice
Parathas/ roti/ frozen parathas
Garlic mayonnaise/ plain mayonnaise
Pickled onions
Lit coal for bbq smoke flavor

MUTTON
RECIPES

1. SEEKH KABAB KADHAI

Cylindrical kababs are tossed in a spicy kadhai masala.

Method:

- In a food processor, blend the minced meat with garlic, ginger, gram flour and all the spices for the marinade. Keep aside for an hour.
- For the gravy, sauté onion in 3 tbsp of oil on medium heat till they turn transparent. Add ginger, garlic, red chili flakes, coriander powder, turmeric powder, cumin powder, tomatoes and green chilies. Turn off the stove.
- Mold the kababs into small cylinders. Shallow fry the kababs on medium heat with 4 tbsp of oil till they are almost cooked.
- Place the kababs in the gravy masala, cook for 10 minutes or more till the oil comes on surface and the tomatoes are soft.
- Serve hot with naan.

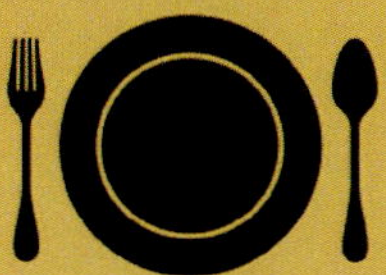

Servings : 6

Preparation time:
1 Hour

Ingredients:

For the seekh kabab:
400g minced mutton/ chicken
1 small onion
3 garlic cloves
Inch of ginger
Few fresh coriander leaves
1 tsp garam masala powder
1 tsp red chili powder
1 tsp coriander powder
½ tsp cumin seeds
1 tsp salt
2 tsp gram flour/ besan

For the gravy:
2 onions sliced
2 tomatoes chopped
4 green chilis with a slit
1 tsp garlic paste
½ tsp turmeric powder
½ tsp coriander powder
½ tsp red chili flakes
½ tsp cumin powder
1 tsp salt
Oil

2. ACHAR GOSHT (PICKLED MUTTON CURRY)

ACHAR GOSHT (PICKLED MUTTON CURRY)

Achar gosht is a spicy, tangy, aromatic pickled mutton curry.

Method:

- In a wok, sauté blended onions in oil on medium flame till they turn transparent.
- In a mortar and pestle, crush cumin seeds, fennel seeds, black pepper, mustard seeds and coriander seeds.
- Add the above spices, black seeds, cinnamon stick, salt, ginger and garlic and pickle oil into the wok. Toss in meat and tomatoes. Cover the lid and let it cook for about 30 minutes or more on low flame till the meat is ready. Add water if the gravy seems to dry.
- Mix in green chilis and lemon juice. Garnish with fresh coriander leaves. Serve hot with naan/ roti.

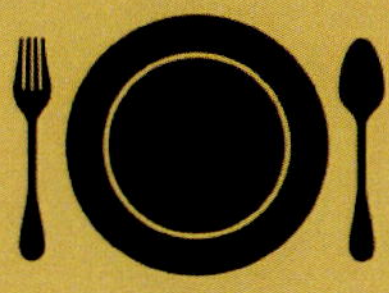

Servings : 6

Preparation time: 1 Hour

Ingredients:

700 g mutton/ chicken pieces
2 medium sized onions blended into paste
4 tomatoes blended
1 tsp garlic chopped
1 tsp ginger chopped
1 tsp red chili powder
½ tsp turmeric powder
1 tsp whole black pepper
1 tsp whole coriander seeds
1 tsp cumin seeds
1 tsp black seeds
1 tsp mustard seeds
1 tsp fennel seeds
4 green chilis slit
1 tbsp lemon juice
Fresh coriander leaves for garnishing
4 tbsp oil
1 ¼ tsp salt
2 tbsp pickle oil

3. MUTTON CHOPS WITH STEAMED VEGETABLES

MUTTON CHOPS WITH STEAMED VEGETABLES

My mum makes these scrumptious mutton chops when I visit her. Steamed broccoli, beans, corn and carrot provide a good source of essential vitamins and antioxidants. My kids love the colorful vegetables and the ability to hold the chops in their hands like chicken drumsticks. If your kids are picky eaters, try making this recipe. It takes no time to present these lovely chops and vegetables on your dinner table.

Method:

- In a bowl, add all the ingredients of the marinade. Mix to form a smooth paste and toss in the chops. Marinate for about 4 hours.
- Season the vegetables with salt and pepper. Steam till they are cooked.
- In a pressure cooker, add the chops and the marinade with half cup of water.
- Cook on low flame after first whistle for 15 minutes or more till the chops are cooked.
- Serve these chops with steamed vegetables and garlic bread/ bun.

Servings : 4 - 6

Preparation time: 30 minutes

Marination time : 4 Hours

Ingredients:

For the marinade:

700 g mutton chops
2 tbsp hot sauce
1 tsp ginger paste
1 tsp garlic paste
1 tbsp lemon juice
1 tsp chaat masala
1 ½ tbsp yogurt
2 tbsp oil
1 ¼ tsp salt

For the steamed vegetables:

1 cup carrot cut into thick slices
1 cup broccoli
1 cup corn
1 cup green beans cut into inch size pieces
3/4 tsp pepper
Salt to taste

4. DUMQEEMA(SMOKED MINCED MEAT)

Servings : 6

Preparation time: 30 minutes

Ingredients:

500g minced mutton
1 medium size tomatoes
1 tsp chopped garlic
1 tsp chopped ginger
1 medium size onion
2 green chilis
2 cardamom
2 cloves
3 whole black pepper corns
1 tsp cumin seeds
1 tsp red chili powder
1 tsp coriander powder
½ tsp turmeric powder
1 tsp garam masala
2 tbsp blended yogurt
1 tbsp lemon

SMOKED MINCED MEAT (DUMQEEMA)

Smoked minced mutton cooked with garam masala.

4 tbsp oil
2 tbsp flour
1 ½ tsp salt
Fried onion slices for garnish
Thinly sliced ginger for garnish
Chopped green chilis for garnish
Lit coal for smoke

Method:

- In a pot, add oil and onions on medium heat followed by whole green chilis. Sauté the onions till they get transparent. Add garlic, ginger, cardamom, cloves and black pepper. Mix in the minced meat and stir for about 2 minutes. Cover with the lid.
- In a blender, blend the tomatoes till it turns into a smooth paste. Pour the tomato paste into the pot. Add coriander powder, red chili powder, turmeric powder and salt. Mix well and cook on low heat for about 10 minutes. If you think the meat is sticking to the pot, add quarter cup of water.
- Pour blended yogurt followed by garam masala powder and lemon juice. Cook for 10 minutes on low heat and add in the flour mixture. Stir for 2 minutes till there is no water left in the pot.
- Place a lit coal on foil paper in the pot. Pour 1 tsp of oil on the coal and close the lid of the pot. Let the minced meat absorb the smoke for about 10 minutes.
- Garnish with chopped green chilis, fried onion and ginger slices. Serve hot with naan.

DESSERTS

1. CHOCOLATE CUPCAKES WITH CREAM CHEESE FROSTING

Chocolate cupcakes are a classic treat. Moist chocolate cupcakes with a delicious cream cheese frosting are loved both by adults and kids.

Method:

- Preheat oven to 175 degrees Celsius.
- Beat together flour, cocoa, baking powder, baking soda, milk, eggs, oil, sugar, salt and vanilla.
- Stir in boiling coffee.
- Line the cupcake tray with cupcake liners. This will make about 20 to 24 cupcakes. Pour in till 2/3 of cupcake liner is filled.
- Bake for 20 minutes or more till done.
- For the frosting, beat together slightly melted butter and cream cheese together. Add in vanilla and milk. Gradually add icing sugar and beat till fluffy.
- After the cupcakes are at room temperature, apply the frosting. Decorate with sprinkles.

Servings : 12

Preparation time: 30 minutes

Ingredients

2 cups sugar
1 3/4 cup all-purpose flour
½ cup cocoa powder
1 ½ tsp baking powder
1 ½ tsp baking soda
1 tsp salt
2 eggs
1 cup milk
½ cup oil
2 tsp vanilla extract
1 cup boiling coffee
For the frosting:
8-ounce butter
8-ounce cream cheese
1 ½ tsp vanilla essence
1 tsp milk
½ cup icing sugar or more

2. JELLY SLICES

JELLY SLICES

There is a common misconception that dentists would avoid all kind of desserts and cariogenic food. Well I can't say about all the dentists but certainly I have a sweet tooth.

Jelly slices are a fusion of biscuit layer, panna cotta layer and a top layer of jelly. A treat for the eyes as well as your taste buds.

Method:

- Crush the biscuits and mix with the butter. Press on any Pyrex dish. Freeze for 20 minutes.
- Dissolve gelatin in 1/2 cup of hot water. Add condensed milk and lemon juice.
- Pour the panna cotta (gelatin mixture) on the biscuit layer and refrigerate till it sets. Dissolve strawberry jelly as per packet instructions. Allow to cool and pour the jelly on top of the panna cotta.
- Place in the fridge till it sets. Cut into pieces and serve.

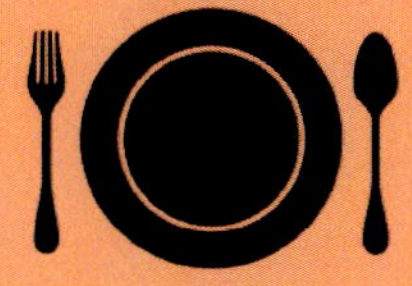

Servings : 10

Preparation time: 30 minutes

Ingredients:

400g sweetened condensed milk
100g butter melted
100g strawberry jelly powder (or any red color jelly)
200g Digestive biscuits
1 tbsp gelatin
1 tbsp lemon juice
½ cup water

3. PANCAKE FOR KIDS

PANCAKE FOR KIDS

On weekends, my kids request me to make special pancakes for them. It is an easy-peasy recipe of simple fluffy pancakes. I pour the batter in a squeezable bottle with a small nozzle and make these amazing shapes for them. They enjoy having these pancakes with fruits, honey, Nutella and cream.

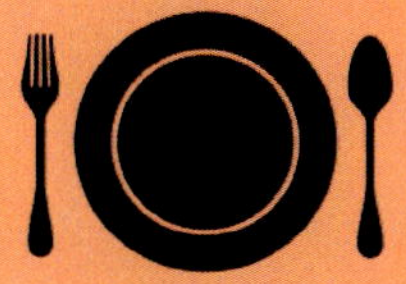

Servings : 3

Preparation time: 15 minutes

Ingredients:

1cup all-purpose flour
1 tsp baking powder
1 tsp sugar
1 egg
1 tbsp olive oil
1 cup milk
1 tsp vanilla essence

Method:

- Beat together egg and sugar for 1 minute.
- Add vanilla essence, flour, baking powder, olive oil and milk. Beat till a smooth thin batter is formed.
- Pour the batter in a squeezable bottle with a nozzle. Grease the pan on medium heat with oil.
- Follow your imagination and make pancakes. Flip the pancakes till light brown on both sides.
- Serve with fruits, Nutella, honey, maple syrup or cream.

Tip: If the batter seems too thick, add few tsps of milk.

4. NUTELLA BROWNIES

NUTELLA BROWNIES

Treat yourself to one of the best 'crunchy from the outside and melt in the mouth texture inside' Nutella brownies.

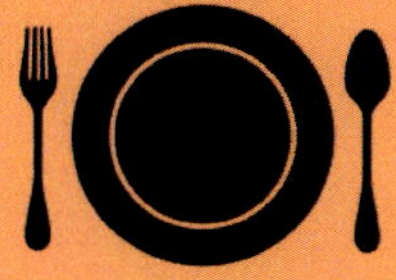

Servings : 6-8

Preparation time: 1 Hour

Ingredients:

12 tbsp Nutella
7 tbsp butter
2 eggs
½ cup sugar
¾ cup flour

Method:

- Preheat the oven to 180 degrees Celsius. In a double boiler, mix butter and Nutella. Keep to cool.
- Whisk together eggs and sugar till the mixture is pale yellow and foamy.
- Add Nutella mixture to the eggs and sugar. Mix in the flour gradually till the batter is smooth and lumps free.
- Bake for 45 minutes till the brownies crack from the surface and are still moist from the inside.
- Serve with vanilla ice cream.

5. PINEAPPLE TOFFEE TRIFLE

PINEAPPLE TOFFEE TRIFLE

This is my version of banoffee pie, instead of bananas I used pineapples. Pineapple toffee trifle is basically comprised of four layers. Biscuit layer, toffee layer, whip cream layer and lastly the pineapple layer. Every bite of this trifle will stimulate all the nerve endings of your tongue.

Method:

- First we will prepare the toffee layer. Take a saucepan. Add butter, brown sugar and condensed milk. Stir the mixture on low heat till its light brown and slightly sticky. Make sure you stir occasionally or else the mixture will stick to the pan. Keep it aside and let it cool.
- Crush the digestive biscuits with your hands about 1 inch pieces roughly. Take a transparent bowl, add half of the biscuits in a layer. Then pour about 3 tbsp of pineapple juice over the biscuit layer just to make it little soggy. Your first layer is ready.
- For the second layer, pour half the toffee mixture over the biscuits followed by half of whip cream. Whip cream is your third layer.
- Then cover the whip cream with pieces of pineapple which will be the fourth layer.
- Repeat the four layers again. Garnish the final top layer with pineapple and strawberries. Adding strawberry brings out the vibrant colors to this dish. Keep it in the fridge for an hour or two. Serve chilled.

Servings : 4

Preparation time: 2 Hours

Ingredients:
70g unsalted butter
10 tbsp brown sugar
½ cup sweet condensed milk
1 cup tinned pineapple pieces
1 cup digestive biscuits
2 cups whip cream
½ cup fresh sliced strawberries
6 tbsp of pineapple juice left in tin

6. KHEER (RICE PUDDING)

Kheer is made of rice boiled in milk. This quick and simple recipe can be tried for any festive occasion.

Method:

- Wash rice and soak for 30 minutes in water. Drain the water and blend the rice till they are roughly crushed.
- Boil milk in a pan and add the crushed rice. Cook on low flame for about 40 minutes stirring occasionally.
- Scrape the sides of the pan and add this dried milk into the pan. The kheer should be thick and the rice cooked well.
- Add the condensed milk and cardamom. Stir and cook for another 5 minutes. There should be no lumps.
- Garnish with almonds.
- You can serve the kheer hot or cold. Refrigerate for an hour before serving.

Servings : 8

Preparation time: 1 Hour

Ingredients:

400g sweetened condensed milk
1 liter milk
¼ cup raw basmati rice
½ tsp cardamom powder
Chopped almonds for garnishing

7. SOOJI KA HALWA (SEMOLINA DESSERT)

SOOJI KA HALWA(SEMOLINA DESSERT)

Semolina dessert known as the famous sooji ka halwa is eaten usually for breakfast with fresh pooris. It is an easy to follow recipe and the halwa tastes just like you get in restaurants. Satisfy your breakfast cravings with homemade halwa.

Method:

- Boil water, baking soda and sugar together with cardamom till all the sugar has dissolved. Add the food color and mix. Keep aside this sugar syrup.
- In a pot, sauté semolina on low heat for 5 minutes. Add ghee/ clarified butter and sauté for 10 minutes or till the semolina changes into light brown. Add the gram flour and mix.
- Gradually add the sugar syrup and mix with the semolina. Keep stirring for 5 minutes. Close the lid and cook for another 10 minutes or more till the water has dried and the ghee can be seen separate from the halwa.
- Garnish with raisins and almonds. Serve with hot pooris.

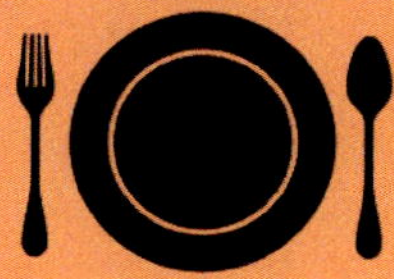

Servings : 6

Preparation time: 30 minutes

Ingredients:

½ cup semolina/ sooji
½ cup ghee/ clarified butter
4 crushed cardamoms
3/4 cup sugar
1 cup water
½ tsp or more orange food colouring
pinch of baking soda
½ tsp gram flour/ besan
Chopped almonds for garnishing
Raisins for garnishing